the LAST YEARS of the 'PEAKS'

'PEAKS'

STEPHEN R. BATTY

LONDON

IAN ALLAN LTD

Introduction

Cover: Class 46 No 46.015 approaches Brightside near Sheffield with the 10.12 Newcastle–Cardiff on 28 February 1977. *L.A. Nixon*

Previous page: Class 45 No 45.034 commences the long descent to Carlisle with the 08.00 St Pancras–Glasgow on 27 April 1976. *J.E. Oxley*

First published 1985

ISBN 0 7110 1493 0

Published by Ian Allan Ltd, Shepperton, Surrey; and printed by Ian Allan Printing Ltd at their works at Coombelands in Runnymede, England.

Describing the recent activities of the 'Peak' class BR/Sulzer 1Co-Co1 locomotives is an interesting and revealing exercise. The 'Peak' class covers four varieties of one design, and each of these clearly demonstrates how time and circumstances can have totally differing results on what are fundamentally identical products put to different uses at different times over a 25 year period. This evolution of the class means that their earlier history must be considered in any review of their most recent activities. After initially undertaking virtually identical duties, the 'Peaks' were then subjected to a mixture of withdrawal, refurbishment and conversion which resulted in the division of the class into four component sub-classes. Indeed, the title of this album needs some qualification for each of those sub-classes: 44, 45/0, 45/1 and 46. The original 10 Class 44 locomotives which gave the name to the class have been extinct since 1980, although two have been privately preserved. Class 45 machines form the bulk of the number, with Class 45/0 consisting of essentially un-modified locomotives retaining steam heating equipment which in some cases has now been isolated. The first withdrawal took place in June 1977, and has been followed by several more up to the present day. However, at the time of writing, these locomotives are still seen at work on all types of freight and passenger duties up and down the country. Naturally, their employment on passenger work tends to be confined to the warmer months of the year, unless steam-heated stock is being hauled. The Class 45/1 locomotives are those which were converted to electrical train heating equipment in the mid-1970s, to fill gaps in motive power requirements until more modern traction is available. At the moment this time is some years ahead, and Class 45/1 locomotives are hard at work on fast express passenger duties. Last of all are the class 46 machines, which are very similar to Class 45/0 but fitted with electrical equipment supplied by a different manufacturer. Despite being the last batch of 'Peaks' to be built, they suffered more rapid withdrawals (the first was in December 1977) than Class 45/0 and finally became extinct in November 1984.

Deciding just when the 'Peaks' entered their last years is thus a difficult question which could be answered equally well from several different viewpoints. Most of the photographs in this album were taken in the 1974–84 period, but much material has been used to illustrate the first 15 years of 'Peak' activity. Whilst Class 44 is extinct (apart from two privately preserved examples), as is Class 46, the '45/0' locomotives are still widely used and the '45/1' machines are being worked harder that at any earlier period in their history. Disregarding the first 45/0 withdrawal in June 1977 (due to collision damage) and two similarly uncharacteristically early withdrawals amongst the 46s, it would seem reasonable to start the photographic story of the last

years of the 'Peaks' in 1980. Many withdrawals occurred during this and the following year (hastened by the economic recession), but, paradoxically, the '45/1s' were involved in a heavy general overhaul programme at this time which would usefully extend their lives by at least ten years. Bearing in mind that the 2,300hp Class 44 finally disappeared in this year, the choice seems a good starting point.

Below: The 15.15 Manchester (Piccadilly)–Harwich passes through sylvan surroundings near Edale behind Class 45/0 No 45.003 on 1 August 1977.   *P.H. Hanson*

History of the Design

The story of the 'Peaks' begins in the mid-1950s, when British Railways engineers were deciding what types of locomotive should be ordered from the various builders under the Pilot Scheme of the BR Modernisation Plan. The London Midland Region management wanted to secure electrification of the West Coast main line (WCML) from Euston to Glasgow, and viewed the use of diesel power as a purely intermediate measure on this important trunk route service. Some experience with diesel operation had already been gained with Nos 10000 and 10001, the LMS-designed Co-Co locomotives, and also with the SR 1Co-Co1 machines Nos 10201, 10202 and 10203. Both of these designs were fitted with English Electric 1,600hp SVT engines, but such an output was clearly inadequate for hauling the fast, heavy trains which would be introduced in the years leading to electrification. Here, the engineers encountered a problem. An engine output of well over 2,000hp was deemed necessary, and very few manufacturers could offer such powerful machinery for railway use. English Electric had in fact developed the 16SVT engine to produce 2,000hp, (as seen in No 10203 from 1954 and in the production D200 series from 1958), but only the Sulzer Company in Switzerland could offer a ready-made 2,300hp installation.

The Sulzer brothers had at this time been involved in producing diesel engines for railway use for over forty years, and had developed the versatile LDA range of engines to cover medium and high-power applications. The London Midland Region (LMR) wanted two types of locomotive under the Modernisation Plan, one for high-power use and a smaller type for lighter duties on all parts of the system. Sulzer could provide both power plants – the six and eight-cylinder in-line units for the smaller locomotives and the much larger double-bank 12-cylinder version for the main-line locomotive. Many parts (eg pistons, liners, connecting rods, bearings) were interchangeable across the LDA range, and these engines had occasionally been built under licence by Sir W.G. Armstrong, Whitworth & Co of Newcastle since 1931. The larger twin-bank engines had appeared in 1938, and covered the 400–2,200hp range by the early 1950s. Very few of these had seen railway service, with a few in use in France and Rumania, but they were the only engines which were

readily available and which had a track record of railway use, albeit at lower power levels than BR wanted ideally. Interchangeability of components and the convenience of an inland manufacturer were strong points in Sulzer's favour. The decision was taken to equip three new Type 4 locomotives with the 2,300hp 12LDA28 pressure-charged engine, with the smaller type 2 and 3 classes having the 6LDA28 and 8LDA28.

10 locomotives were ordered under Class 'C' of the 'Pilot Lot' order in November 1955, to be built by BR at their Derby works. At the time they were the most powerful diesel locomotives to be ordered from BR workshops. Nearly four years passed before the first locomotive, numbered D1, appeared in the summer of 1959, and its appearance created much interest among observers and railwaymen alike. The massive appearance gave some clues to design difficulties which had had to be overcome during the intervening four years. Originally it had been intended to use a pair of three-axle bogies of the Co-Co arrangement, but such was the weight of the finished product that an extra trailing axle had to be fitted to keep the axle loading within the Civil Engineer's limits. Bogie design generally was almost identical to that of the Southern Region's 10201–3 locomotives, being made from steel plates rivetted and welded together. Side play was allowed on the centre driven axle only, the outer two being fixed. A very stiff body construction was obtained by using a lattice-girder construction and masses of continuous sheet steel body panels. The roof was completely removable above the power unit to facilitate easy maintenance. The engine's twin crank shafts were both geared onto a common output shaft on which was mounted the Crompton Parkinson generator, the largest of its type in Europe at the time. A step-up gear ratio was fitted between the crankshafts and the generator, allowing the ideal combination of a low-speed (750 rev/min) engine and a high-speed, and hence smaller, generator running at 1,080 rev/min. This 10-pole machine produced 1,531 KW at 580V, 2640A and had its cooling fan and commutator fitted to the driven end of the shaft, with the 8-pole 90KW auxiliary generator mounted on the free end. This latter item had its windings recessed into those of the main generator, an arrangement which saved overall length on the power

unit. A Stone-Vapor train heating boiler producing 2,750 lb/hr of steam was fitted at the No 2 end, along with two 400gal water tanks alongside and a further 540gal tank underslung between the bogies. The new locomotives were built up from several sub-assemblies from the Derby workshops, which helped to achieve a good spread of work during the steam-diesel changeover period.

The Derby engineers had been given a fairly free hand in the design, layout and appearance of the new locomotives, hence the more than passing visual resemblance to the LMS-produced twins, Nos 10000 and 10001. Popular approval was soon given to the looks of the new Sulzer Type 4, with its clean sides, neat grille panels and attractive green livery. But the decision to name these 10 locomotives after various English and Welsh mountains not only christened the entire class (including future members) for all their working lives, it was also seen by some as a pointer to their most unwelcome feature-weight. An all-up figure of 138ton could not be compared to the 78ton of the similarly powerful 'Warship' class diesel-hydraulics then being put in service on the Western Region. By this time a decision had been taken to order a further 147 'Peaks' from Derby and Crewe works, using the latest 2,500hp development of the Sulzer engine, the 12LDA28-B. Consideration was given to fitting electrical train heating (ETH) equipment to the new locomotives, and so doing away with the train heating boiler and water tanks. This was estimated to give a weight saving of about 20ton, allowing the use of a Co-Co axle arrangement as originally intended. Nothing came of these proposals, although of course ETH equipment was fitted to Class 45/1 many years later.

But back to No D1 and her early life with the LMR. The new class was capable of working in multiple with locomotives equipped by British Thomson-Houston, English Electric and Crompton Parkinson, and was intended to be able to haul passenger trains of 660ton at 74mph. Crewe depot received the first 10 locomotives (facilities were not completed at Camden, in London) with the intention of working passenger and parcels duties along the full length of the WCML. In early June 1959, D1 went from Derby (where she was technically on loan from Crewe) to Preston for trials on a particularly difficult obtuse crossing, and then ran light engine to Carlisle for a naming ceremony on 12 July. All the locomotives in the D1–D10 series were fitted with their nameplates during construction, the official naming ceremonies taking place in due course after they entered traffic. Soon afterwards both D1 and D2 returned to Derby for new pistons to be fitted. By late August both were back in service, but still operating from Derby, where a close watch could be kept on their performance. Their work was confined to Manchester trains, as the Civil Engineer had not yet agreed to their use southwards along the Midland

main line to St Pancras. Most of their duties were anything but arduous, and did not make heavy demands on their capabilities. Even on these jobs, they were hampered by severe speed restrictions at Manchester (Central) due to their weight and bogie arrangement. The rest of 1959 was spent on the Midland lines, but by early 1960, when all 10 numbers of the initial order were delivered, crew training on the WCML began from Crewe, Edge Hill, Longsight and Carlisle (Upperby) depots. No D2 was actually delivered with an uprated 2,500hp engine which was allied to re-geared traction motors capable of giving a maximum speed of well over 90mph. Several test runs were conducted, culminating in a maximum of 110mph whilst hauling a three-coach train. After being used for pre-electrification track investigation work, D2 was derated to 2,300hp in February 1963.

Whilst being employed on these passenger duties, a problem with the traction motors came to light. Due to the arrangement of the field weakening switching arrangement, traction motor flashovers at higher speeds became a serious problem. Modifications were done to reduce the flashovers, but these incurred a penalty of reduced performance in the upper speed range. The problem also occurred in the remainder of the 'Peaks', from D11 onwards, but by the time these machines were available the WCML duties had been taken over by the English Electric Type 4 (Class 40) locomotives. Consequently the 'Peaks' never saw their intended duty on London (Euston)–Glasgow turns, and the 10 original locomotives were relegated to freight work based on Toton depot from the early 1960s. Work is still being done to eliminate this problem, which affects the Class 45/1 locomotives more than the lighter-loaded, slower running Class 45/0.

As more 'Peaks' were introduced, the LMR gained more experience in the problems and general day-to-day running of the fleet. The equipment layout within the engine room was rather crowded, and gave some headaches to the MPD staff who had to remove and replace various items either for maintenance or due to failures. One early modification involved the removable roof section. Cylinder head work necessitated removal of the complete roof in order to gain access, and this naturally involved a lot of time and effort being expended just to get at the work area. In the mid-1960s this roof was redesigned into a split-section assembly, greatly simplifying the 'top-end' jobs. The vacuum brake exhauster, the air compressor (for the locomotive brake), brake control cubicle and rotary converter were all crammed together at the No 1 end. Removal and replacement of these items, or the nose-mounted traction motor blowers, involved hours of work in juggling the equipment out of its normal service position, into the cab and out through the cab door. The No 2 end housed the train heating equipment, perhaps the most troublesome area on diesel locomotives generally, and the radiator and fuel tanks were placed at the No 1 end. Roof-mounted header tanks for coolant and fuel were awkward to reach, but the radiators and fan caused few problems. This latter item was electrically driven, and speed-controlled by thermostats which sensed the coolant temperature.

The early locomotives had start contactors operated by compressed air to use the generator as a starter motor to turn the Sulzer engine from rest, and experience soon exposed a weakness in this starting scheme.

Before the engine could be turned over, the combined pump set (fuel, oil, coolant), rotary converter and compressor had all to be put in service, their motors taking power from the locomotive's lead-acid batteries. This electrical load on the batteries was high and they had to work to the limit of their capacity to run the compressor to produce an air supply of 40 psi, and provide power to turn the engine. A first-start failure often left the locomotive stranded, as the batteries were then incapable of running all these items for a second attempt.

A starting system using electromagnetic starting contactors was introduced which solved this problem.

Mention must now be made of the further order made by BR for the remainder of the 'Peaks', Nos D11–D193. All these were to be fitted with the uprated 2,500hp engine (the 12LDA28-B), and originally the last 76 were to have electrical equipment supplied by Brush of Loughborough. This was due to Crompton Parkinson's workshops being fully committed at the time, although soon afterwards the order was reduced to 56 locomotives to allow Brush to produce their highly successful Co-Co design for BR, now familiar as Class 47. Extra output was obtained from the engine by the use of intercooling, where the combustion air passes through a cooler fitted between the pressure-charger outlet and cylinder-head inlet valves. The cooler, denser nature of the air allows a greater weight of oxygen to be fed into the engine, hence more fuel can be burned and more power produced. The intercooler reduces the air inlet temperature to the engine, hence the exhaust gas temperature is kept below a value above which expensive materials would have to be used for exhaust valves, manifolds, pressure-charger blading and casings etc.

The engines for this order were all supplied by Vickers of Barrow-in-Furness, whereas the 2,300hp units had come from Winterthur in Switzerland. Pressure chargers, also of Swiss origin on the original locomotives, were to be supplied by the de Havilland company. In order to give the class a more mixed traffic capability, a different traction motor was fitted, and the tractive effort increased from 50,000lb (maximum) and 29,100lb (continuous) to 55,000lb and 30,000lb respectively. The locomotives of the D1–D10 series were all modified to these ratings in due course.

Cab front design was altered in view of the lack of any need for communication between two locomotives when double-heading, itself a rare event. D1–D10 had been provided with gangway connecting doors and headcode indicator discs and lamps, the two central disc assemblies being slightly offset from the centre of the doors. The elimination of the doors took place during the construction of the new order, and several variations emerged. Locomotives D11–D31 and D68–D107 were built with two box-type roller blind indicators, one at each side of the nose-end. Remaining locomotives were produced using a one or two-piece four-character display placed in the centre of the nose. In later years all these indicators were deemed redundant, and were replaced with the twin marker lights with which the survivors are fitted today. The replacement was usually done at a works overhaul, but collision damage often meant an unscheduled replacement being quickly carried out. Cases did exist where a locomotive carried two different types of cab end at the same time for this reason. Even today, one or two cab ends still carry the remains of their original lamp brackets.

Locomotives equipped by Brush were fitted with that company's TG160-60 generator, providing 1,650KW at 760V, 2100A. The auxiliary generator was a TG69-28 giving 47.5KW at 110V, 432A. Traction motors were TM73-68 Mk 3. All were built without nose doors and with a central four-digit route indicator. Other major differences were the use of a Spanner Mk 3 train-heating boiler, and the replacement of the electrically-driven radiator fan by a hydrostatically-powered system. Electrical supplies for control and lighting equipment were taken directly from the auxiliary generator, whereas the Crompton Parkinson system involved using a rotary converter.

Building was intended to take place at Crewe and Derby workshops, with the latter having the larger order. Pressure of work resulted in part of the Derby order being transferred to Crewe, and the locomotives entered service (not in numerical order) over a two year period from autumn 1960. The depots at Cricklewood, Derby and Toton received most of the new locomotives, and the Midland main line from St. Pancras was quickly taken over by the 'Peaks'. They spread their influence to the Leeds area in early 1961, when D11 and D14 were allocated to Neville Hill for crew-training duties to Glasgow, Newcastle and Liverpool. D93 went to Bristol and D13 to Glasgow for similar purposes, and the summer of that year saw 'Peaks' displacing 'Jubilees', 'Royal Scots' and ex-LNER 'Pacifics' from the Leeds–Glasgow, Liverpool–Newcastle and Newcastle–Bristol services. Locomotives D11–D16 were allocated to Leeds (Holbeck) in 1961, and all except D11 (now No 45.122) were still at the depot when its allocation was dispersed in 1978. New Class 46 locomotives, as the Brush-equipped members of the class became known in later years, were delivered from late 1961 and initially worked from Derby and Gateshead. These Derby 'Peaks' worked on the Northeast–Southwest (NESW) services, and the Gateshead locos reached the length of the ECML as well as Leeds and Liverpool. Some were allocated to Edinburgh (Haymarket) for a short while.

Various problems came to light during these early years of operation, and although most have been solved over the years, some do persist today. Naturally, as a fleet of locomotives progresses through its working life, new problems will crop up from time to time due to ageing and changing patterns of use. An early modification which was clearly visible concerned the filling point for the train-heating boiler water tanks. This was placed on the slope of the roof at No 2 end, and access to the filler and its cover was gained by means of three steps in the body side. The gradual disappearance of station water cranes and, more importantly, the arrival of overhead electrification equipment, resulted in the filler being transferred to the solebar and the cover and steps being plated over. Many covers had actually been lost along the line, flying off at speed.

The 2,500hp engines stood up well in service, but problems did occur. Pressure-charger turbine blade failures were blamed on high exhaust temperatures and vibration, and were cured by fitting lacing wires through the blade tips. Twenty locomotives were affected before the modification was completed. Some crankcase fractures were found, (which Sulzer did attribute to the uprating), and combustion problems occurred due to the injectors becoming carboned up during periods of idling on partial-load operation. Cylinder head valve fractures took place, but this was solved by replacing the existing chromed valves with a plain variety. Leakage of coolant past cylinder liner joints is still a problem today, but cylinder head fractures around the core plugs were cured by a new design of cylinder head being employed. Coolant circulates from the cylinder blocks up to the cylinder heads via external transition bushes fitted between the two, and leakage from these bushes caused headaches for years. Several redesigns of the bushes were done to try and cure the fault, and it is only in recent years that success has been achieved.

Cylinder head studs have shown a tendency to fracture, and this remains so at the present time. However, modern ultrasonic testing (which can be done without taking the locomotive out of service) allows the detection of any fault before failure takes place. Exhaust system bellows pieces are troublesome, and replacements are becoming difficult to obtain. This problem could be solved by finding an alternative supplier, which may involve some re-designing of the components, or by eliminating the bellows pieces altogether – trials towards this end have taken place, but no outcome has yet been reached. A persistent problem of recent years concerns the engine lubricating oil cooler. Pitting of

the water side of the tubes, probably due to cavitation erosion, has resulted in replacement of the tube stacks where necessary. Although the cooler has more heat to dissipate than on the earlier engines, it is not thought that the uprated performance has any bearing on the problem, especially after over 20 years in service.

The main generators have given some cause for concern in recent years. Cases of burst armature banding were eliminated by re-banding with fibreglass during overhaul, and earth faults due to broken brushes have been cleared up. High resistance electrical joints in the armature have caused local burn-outs, particularly if the locomotive has been overloaded for any reason. Hairline cracking of traction motor shafts was discovered during the 1960s and rectified by redesigning the shafts. Electrical problems here still persist despite the improvements designed into the traction motors for Classes 45 and 46 during construction. Flashovers still occur, and during the late 1970s the frequency amongst the Class 45/1 machines reached 80/year plus a further 20–30 cases of damaged axles, gears and bearings. This constituted the highest group of failures in the class, but the problems are expected to be cleared up as the locomotives are overhauled at Derby or Crewe. Traction motor blowers suffer due to the dirty environment of the cab nose ends, and excessive commutator wear was identified in the 1960s. All the auxiliary equipment motors have an appetite for carbon brushes, especially the two-brush Crompton variety – those supplied by the Brush company were fitted with four carbon brushes, and wear rates were lower.

Bogie fractures occur on the side frames at various positions, usually just behind one of the crossmembers. The cracks are kept under observation until a length of 3in is reached, when works attention to the bogie is required. Fractures at the axebox cut-outs are regarded as very serious, and the loco is taken out of service immediately. This has caused some loss of availability in the past, as the bogies would often fail between works visits for planned overhaul. Perhaps the most significant improvement here was the removal, for a trial period only in 1971, of the rotational stops and side control buffers. Track curvature of less than the minimum radius of 5 chains for which the bogies were designed was thought to be a potential cause of the problem, and removal of these items did indicate that some easing of the cracking problem was possible. Accordingly this was done, allowing the 'Peaks' to traverse curves of only 3 chains radius – the absolute minimum possible for the class. Interestingly, the 'Peak' bogie is very similar to that fitted to the English Electric Class 40, but the two are not interchangeable.

Braking troubles have been few. An early problem concerned sparks from the brakeblocks igniting accumulated deposits of oil and grease on the bogies.

This was traced to the locomotive brake being applied too much in advance of the train brake, resulting in the 138ton machine being pushed against its own brakes and so causing brake block pyrotechnics. Modifications to the braking scheme eliminated the problem. Brake slack adjusters still suffer from wear problems (and are also difficult to reach), and some problems exist today in ensuring a supply of spares. Brake hanger suspension bolts occasionally fail, resulting in the loss of the associated brakeblock. Brake block wear is also high, depending on the type of duty being performed.

Delivery of the Crompton-Parkinson equipped machines was completed in January 1962, and the last of the Brush locomotives appeared one year later. The 'Peaks' settled down to passenger and mixed traffic duties between London (St Pancras) and Leeds, Leeds and Glasgow via Carlisle, Liverpool and Newcastle and Newcastle to Bristol via Birmingham. These were their regular territories, but 'Peaks' were frequent visitors to other termini and routes well away from their home depots. Multiple working was found to be unnecessary, and the jumper connections fitted for this purpose were removed during works visits. The first 10 locomotives were by this time employed only on freight duties in the Nottingham area, and their train-heating equipment was duly removed. When withdrawals commenced in 1976, the redundant members of the class were 'cannibalised' to keep ailing Class 45 locomotives in service. During 1965 a refurbishment programme for locomotives D11–D193 was initiated, when the Brush company received a contract to cover all these machines. Lack of BR workshop capacity made this necessary, and the programme was completed during 1969. Rail blue livery was applied during this period, when the original BR 'Passenger Green' was replaced by an unbroken coat of blue and full nose end treatment in yellow.

What will probably turn out to be the only major modification programme concerning the 'Peaks' commenced in 1973. BR's increasing fleet of electrically-heated passenger stock demanded the conversion of an appropriate number of locomotives from conventional steam-heating equipment to the new apparatus. As far as the 'Peaks' were concerned, this meant converting 50 locomotives mainly for use on the St Pancras–Sheffield service. (This new upgraded service was to prove an arduous job, involving fast trains on a route with many speed restrictions and hence many variations in engine power output). A Brush BL100-30 Mk 3 electric train heating auxiliary alternator and rectifier was fitted, and the control equipment was located in the space vacated by the redundant steam generator. Supplies for the locomotive control and lighting equipment, previously taken from the rotary converter, were modified to be taken from this alternator via a set of rectifiers controlled by an electronic voltage

regulator. The bogies were slightly affected by the conversion too, as the modified locomotives had all steam-heating pipework removed and replaced by extra cabling. The TOPS renumbering scheme was applied to the 'Peaks' from this time, resulting in the 2,300hp machines (Nos D1–D10) becoming Class 44, the Crompton-Parkinson 2,500hp locomotives (Nos D11–D137) Class 45, and the Brush fleet (Nos D138–D193) Class 46. Class 46 was deemed to be non-standard, the Class 44 locos were essentially freight haulers only, hence the ETH rebuilding programme drew upon members of Class 45. Delivery commenced in March 1973 when D96 emerged as the first of a new sub-class 45/1, No 45.101, and was completed in July 1975 with No 45.150 (D78). The work was done separately from works overhauls and the locomotives were chosen in non-numerical order to get the fleet in service as soon as possible.

Although the '45/1' machines performed their tasks capably, their availability fell seriously during the later 1970s. The problems were examined in 1978, when the previous year's operations had revealed a casualty rate of 10,000 miles/casualty against a target figure of 13,000 miles/casualty. Availablity had fallen to 65% compared to an all-class 'Peak' figure of 78% in 1970. No evidence existed to show that the ETH conversion was responsible for any problems, indeed the opposite effect could reasonably be expected. Well-known problem areas (as already noted) were identified, but at the time it was not felt that these could be cured during the remaining life of the locomotives. As the 45/1s were expected to be in service on the Midland main line until replaced by HST sets in 1986, it was decided that measures must be taken to improve their reliability and availability. Four options were considered:

1 Rehabilitate the Class 45/1 locomotives at their next scheduled overhaul, regardless of the overhaul classification.
2 Relegate all Class 45s to easier jobs and replace them with Class 47/4 locomotives. (At the time these latter were felt to be under-utilised on Class 1 passenger work.)
3 Wait for HSTs to enter service on the WR, so releasing Class 50 locomotives for possible LMR use.
4 Continue as at present, using other classes to share the work.

Option 1 was chosen, and a Heavy General Overhaul (HGO) programme commenced in the same year. The work was undertaken by Derby, although the last 11 were completed at Crewe in 1983/84. By this time their long monopoly of the Midland line had been ended by the arrival of HST sets some four years earlier than anticipated at the start of the HGO programme. Nevertheless, due to changing economic forces throughout the nation (and BR), more work had been found for the 'Peaks'. The trans-Pennine services via Leeds and Huddersfield had been in the doldrums for some time, and these were to be revitalised by the removal of the ageing DMU fleet and the provision of a fast, locomotive-hauled service over routes which would provide improved passenger loadings. These new services ran between Liverpool, Llandudno and Bangor in the west and Newcastle and Scarborough in the north-east, with Class 45/1 'Peaks' sharing duties with Class 47/4 locomotives. Once again the 'Peaks' have an arduous task, due mainly to the geographical nature of the duties. All the locomotives are based at Toton depot, near Nottingham, and only Gateshead, Longsight and Allerton depots can provide anything more than inspection facilities should problems occur. Unfortunately, the reliability of locomotives on this service has suffered recently, but work is in hand to improve matters. This is not to decry the efforts of the operating staff – a glance at the amount of work involved in scheduled examinations alone, regardless of breakdown problems, will show how much effort is needed to keep the fleet in order – but this is the sort of problem which arises in keeping an ageing fleet of locomotives in service on a system which demands high mileage, availability and performance many miles from the parent depot.

Members of Class 46 were transferred from the LMR to the WR from 1971, to replace the fast-disappearing diesel-hydraulic locomotives. 'Peaks' went to Bristol in that year, and in 1972 Plymouth (Laira) received some ex-ER machines. By the mid-1970s they were also operating from Cardiff, hauling passenger and freight trains over most parts of the WR and also appearing on many inter-regional duties. This did not last for long though – by the end of 1980 all had been reallocated to Gateshead depot and many were placed in store whilst the economic recession raged during 1981. Class 45/0 locomotives were active on all duties in the mid-1970s from Cricklewood, Toton, Tinsley, Leeds (Holbeck) and York, but the Holbeck locos were dispersed in April 1978, the York locos in May 1979 and the Cricklewood allocation by May 1982, leaving the class divided between Tinsley and Toton depots.

Apart from the scrapping of No 45.067 in June 1977 after collision damage suffered near Ilkeston whilst hauling a Nottingham–Glasgow express, withdrawals did not commence until late 1980. As already mentioned, the economic climate took a hand and decided the fate of several 'Peaks', particularly during 1981. The last Class 44s in active service, Nos 44.004 *Great Gable,* 44.007 *Ingleborough* and 44.008 *Penyghent* were withdrawn in November 1980, and by the end of 1981 a total of 18 Class 45/0 and 20 Class 46 had disappeared. Withdrawals amongst Class 45/0 reduced over 1983–84, but the ranks of Class 46 survivors were steadily thinned down until the final five examples were withdrawn from Gateshead on 25

November 1984 (Nos 46.011/025/026/035/045). As previously described, the Class 45/1 'Peaks' are hard at work from Toton depot, and this sub-class will undoubtedly soldier on to become the last representatives of the class to remain in service. The big question, of course, is when will the 'Peaks' become extinct? Present forecasts point to their demise coming when electrification of the ECML displaces the HST sets necessary to take over their duties, which theoretically will occur when the '45/1' locomotives approach the end of the 15-year lifespan following their 1978–84 heavy general overhauls. This refers mainly to their present trans-Pennine duties, and it remains to be seen when 'Peaks' of any variety become displaced from the many other duties on which they are found today. Further electrification work (if it ever comes to fruition) will have a strong bearing upon their future, but as only the East Anglian scheme has been approved at present, this prospect does not present an immediate threat. More likely is the withdrawal of individual machines where remaining life expectancy does not justify the costly replacement of failed, worn-out or damaged major components, or withdrawal of locomotives to provide a stock of spares to keep the remainder of the fleet in service.

The 'Peaks' do not have the charisma of the now extinct 'Deltics', those temperamental thoroughbreds which bellowed up and down the ECML and did much to improve services from their 1960 level and then hold their own right up to the HST era. Nor do they have the individuality attached to the also extinct WR diesel-hydraulic fleet, which all had excellent power/weight ratios but which suffered early withdrawal precisely because they were too individual compared to the rest of the BR diesel fleet. Perhaps the 'Peaks' should be described as 'steady horses', locomotives which have coped well with all tasks put before them and which have given value for money over a 25-year period that may well run to 35 years.

Enthusiasts should remember that the 'Peaks' were the first single-engined diesel-electric locomotives with sufficient power available to allow passenger journey times to be substantially reduced, much as happened (on a more dramatic scale) with the 'Deltics' and HSTs of later years. It would be sad if our attention was drawn to these locomotives only at the eleventh hour before their ultimate demise, as so often happens with modern forms of rail traction. I hope that readers will find the text of this album sufficiently informative and the photographs interesting enough to stimulate interest in the 'Peaks' during their coming last years.

The preparation of this album has been made especially enjoyable by the people most closely concerned with providing the essential material. Mr C.A. Hughes, LMR Diesel Traction Engineer, and his colleague Peter Meredith, both provided a wealth of first-hand experience concerning the design and operation of the 'Peaks' from their inception up to the present day. Much previously-unpublished information regarding failures, problems and maintenance activities etc, was readily discussed and gave a fascinating insight to the job of running today's fleet of 'Peaks'. The assistance given by these gentlemen was invaluable, and I am extremely grateful for their co-operation.

Thanks are due to the Management Committee of the Railway Correspondence & Travel Society for permission to use material published in the 'Railway Observer' over the years. Mr T.C. McKenna made available his large collection of journals and magazines for my use, many photographers contributed from their collections, Linda Bradshaw transformed my appalling handwritten sheets into first-class typescript and my wife Andrea occasionally found herself being hauled off in search of 'Peaks' – to all these people, I say 'thank you'.

Below: The last locomotive in the 'Peak' number series No 46.056 (formerly D193), seen on the wheel lathe at Thornaby during Easter 1981. *B.J. Nicolle*

Maintaining the 'Peaks'

The amount of work involved in keeping the 'Peaks' in good running order is immense. This is not due to any particular difficulties or problems associated solely with the 'Peaks', but is in general keeping with the needs of a fleet of hard-worked, 1950s-designed locomotives at work on today's railway system. A casual reading of the maintenance and repair schedules which describe the tasks undertaken at BRE Works and at the traction maintenance depots (TMD) is a sobering experience. All items of equipment, from large sections of bodywork and components of the engine/generator power unit down to the smallest electrical contactor or pipework union, are scrutinised on a regular time-based cycle of examinations and overhaul. It is impossible to describe these jobs in any but the very briefest of terms, and the following notes are intended to give only the bare outline of these activities.

Attention within BRE Works is given every 8,000 hours, with TMD examinations taking place after 55hr ('A' exam), 275 hr ('B' exam), 825 hr ('C' exam), 1,650 hr ('D' exam) and 4,950 hr ('E' exam). These intervals allow some latitude to cope with variations in TMD capacity, due to varying workloads and diagram arrangement of the locomotives etc. The 'E' examination is intended to fall mid-way between works visits, which from 1984 will be concentrated on BRE Derby Works. The hours figure is computed from the TOPS diagrams, and is essentially the total number of hours spent by the locomotive in motion. No account is taken of time spent with the engine idling between diagrams. During an 8,000 hr works overhaul, a 'standard' repair is given to the power unit, bogies, traction motors and train heating equipment, but the locomotive body and various pieces of auxiliary equipment receive a light repair on the first, an intermediate repair at the next 8,000 hr overhaul, followed by a further light repair and eventually a general repair at the fourth works visit. Items covered by a body overhaul include all auxiliary motors, control contactors, solenoids, relays and cubicle equipment, traction motor cables, wheelslip control gear, AWS equipment, reversing equipment, ETH apparatus (if fitted), train heating boiler and tanks (if fitted), radiator, formerly radiator hydrostatic fan drive (Class 46 only), brake gear, cab and fittings, all pipework, fuel tanks and fire extinguishing equipment.

Examinations are carried out at the TMDs at the intervals noted above. Each exam includes those carried out under previous schedules, ie a 'D' exam will include all items previously checked at 'A', 'B' and 'C' examinations. Very briefly, these schedules cover the following tasks:

'A' Examination Renewal of consumable items, eg top up fuel tanks and lubricating oil levels. Visual inspection of tyres, brake blocks and train heating boiler if fitted. Brake blocks can wear rapidly, and these must be checked frequently. Wheel tyres generally last about 8,000 hrs, but their condition can dictate the need for a bogie overhaul.

'B' Examination The locomotive must be placed over a pit to ensure that a thorough examination and lubrication of the bogies and brake gear can be done. Tyres are given a more rigorous check, and the brake equipment is tested. Batteries are topped up, and a sample of engine lubricating oil is taken for analysis. The results will give information regarding the state of the engine, and indicate if any major remedial work may soon be necessary. Some engine compartment cleaning is done, and the train heating boiler may be acid-cleaned.

'C' Examination A visual check of all auxiliary motors is carried out, noting any signs of flashover or overheating and replacing any worn brushes. Traction motor brush length is checked. Fuel, oil and air filters are changed and engine oil is again sampled. Further checking of the tyre wear is done, and in situ cleaning of the bogies and underframe takes place.

'D' Examination Engine lubricating oil is cleaned or replaced. Fuel injectors are changed and the batteries are cleaned and charged as required. All electrical contactors are examined. Fire extinguishers are weighed, and replaced if necessary.

'E' Examination The major job here is to lift the body clear of the bogies to allow a thorough examination of all exposed equipment, and particularly the changing of brake cylinders and slack adjusters. All motor bearings are lubricated and all auxiliary switches and interlocks are checked.

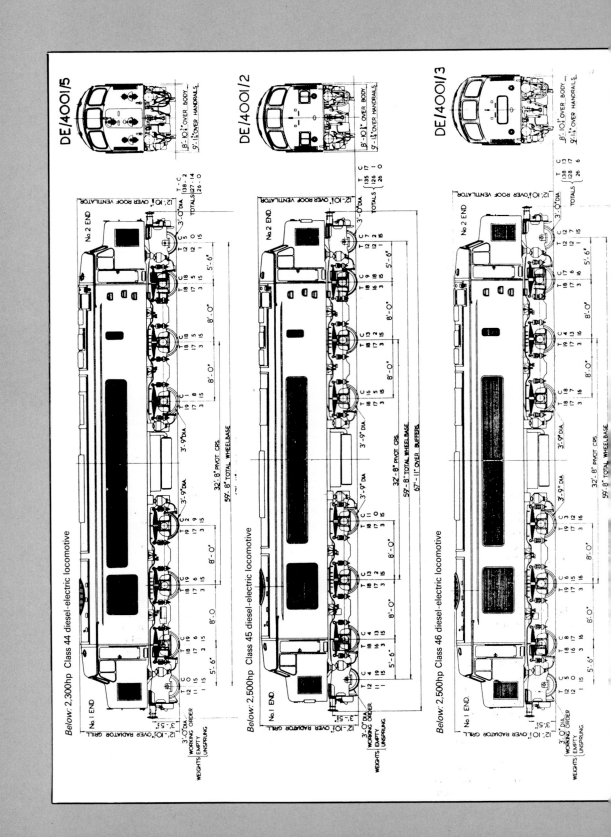

DE/4001/5

8'-0½" OVER BODY
9'-1½" OVER HANDRAILS

12'-10½" OVER ROOF VENTILATOR

No 2 END

3'-0" DIA

	T	C
	12	0	15

TOTALS { 138 · 2 / 127 · 14 / 26 · 0 }

No 1 END

Below: 2,300hp Class 44 diesel-electric locomotive

12'-10½" OVER RADIATOR GRILL

3'-0" DIA

WORKING ORDER / EMPTY / UNSPRUNG

WEIGHTS { EMPTY

3'-5½"

5'-6"   8'-0"   8'-0"   8'-0"   8'-0"   8'-0"   5'-6"
32'-8" TOTAL WHEELBASE
59'-6" TOTAL WHEELBASE

3'-9" DIA

DE/4001/2

8'-0" OVER BODY
9'-1⅛" OVER HANDRAILS

12'-10½" OVER ROOF VENTILATOR

No 2 END

3'-0" DIA

TOTALS { 135 · 1 / 126 · 1 / 26 · 0 }

No 1 END

Below: 2,500hp Class 45 diesel-electric locomotive

12'-10½" OVER RADIATOR GRILL

3'-0" DIA

WORKING ORDER / EMPTY / UNSPRUNG

WEIGHTS { EMPTY

3'-5½"

5'-6"   8'-0"   8'-0"   8'-0"   8'-0"   8'-0"   5'-6"
32'-8" PIVOT CRS.
59'-8" TOTAL WHEELBASE
67'-11" OVER BUFFERS

3'-9" DIA

DE/4001/3

8'-10½" OVER BODY
9'-1¼" OVER HANDRAILS

12'-10½" OVER ROOF VENTILATOR

No 2 END

3'-0" DIA

TOTALS { 138 · 7 / 128 · 17 / 26 · 6 }

No 1 END

Below: 2,500hp Class 46 diesel-electric locomotive

12'-10½" OVER RADIATOR GRILL

3'-0" DIA

WEIGHTS { EMPTY

5'-6"   8'-0"   8'-0"   8'-0"   8'-0"   8'-0"   5'-6"
32'-8" PIVOT CRS.
59'-8" TOTAL WHEELBASE

3'-9" DIA

Technical Particulars of the Peaks as built

	Class 44	Class 45	Class 46
Original BR numbers	D1–D10	D11–D137	D138–D193
Weight in working order	138 ton	135 ton	138 ton
Engine: Type	Sulzer 12LDA–28	Sulzer 12LDA–28B	Sulzer 12LDA–28B
Description	12 cyl, 4 stroke	12 cyl, 4 stroke	12 cyl, 4 stroke
	2,300 hp at 750 rev/min	2,500 hp at 750 rev/min	2,500 hp at 750 rev/min
Compression ratio	12.85:1	12.85:1	12.85:1
Firing order	A bank: 2-4-1-5-3-6	A bank: 2-4-1-5-3-6	A bank: 2-4-1-5-3-6
	B bank: 1-5-3-6-2-4	B bank: 1-5-3-6-2-4	B bank: 1-5-3-6-2-4
Tractive effort (max)	50,000 lb	55,000 lb	55,000 lb
(continuous)	29,100 lb	30,000 lb	31,600 lb
Main generator	Crompton Parkinson CG426A1	Crompton Parkinson CG426A1	Brush TG 160–60
Continuous rating	2,640A, 580V, 1,080 rev/min	2,640A, 580V, 1,080 rev/min	1,750A, 945V, 1,080 rev/min
Auxiliary generator	CP CAG 252A1	CP CAG 252A1	Brush TAG 69–28
Continuous rating	410A, 220V, 1,080 rev/min	410A, 220V, 1,080 rev/min	432A, 110V, 1,080 rev/min
Traction motors	CP C171B1	CP C172A1	Brush TM 73–68 MK.3
Continuous rating	440A, 580V	445A, 615V	700A, 392V
Rail hp at continuous rating	1,800	2,000	1,962
Braking; Loco/train	Air/Vacuum	Air/Vacuum	Air/Vacuum
Brake force, % of loco weight in full working order	76.7%	78%	76.5%
Maximum Speed	90 mph	90 mph	90 mph
Train heating equipment	Stone Vapor OK 4625, 2,750 lb/h	Stone Vapor OK 4625, 2,750 lb/h	Stone Vapor OK 4625, 2,750 lb/h
Fuel oil capacity (engine + b/r)	840 gal	840 gal	835 gal
Boiler water capacity	1,340 gal	1,340 gal	1,340 gal
Cooling water capacity	345 gal	345 gal	345 gal

'Peak' Names

A total of 37 'Peak' locomotives have carried names. The Class 44 machines were delivered new with nameplates already attached, and the remaining locomotives were named at ceremonies between September 1961 and October 1967. Of the named Class 45/46 locomotives, all but five remain in service at the time of writing. Many of the names were taken directly from withdrawn steam locomotives of the 'Patriot' and 'Royal Scot' classes, eg *The Royal Pioneer Corps, Royal Engineer;* some were updated during the transfer, eg *The Royal Warwickshire Regiment* became *The Royal Warwickshire Fusiliers;* and some were completely new, eg *The Royal Marines.*

The particulars are as follows:

BR No	TOPS No	Name	Date Named	Withdrawn
D1	44.001	*Scafell Pike*	9/59	10/76
D2	44.002	*Helvellyn*	10/59	4/79
D3	44.003	*Skiddaw*	10/59	7/76
D4	44.004	*Great Gable*	10/59	11/80
D5	44.005	*Cross Fell*	11/59	4/78
D6	44.006	*Whernside*	12/59	1/77
D7	44.007	*Ingleborough*	12/59	11/80
D8	44.008	*Penyghent*	12/59	11/80
D9	44.009	*Snowdon*	12/59	5/79
D10	44.010	*Tryfan*	2/60	5/77
D49	45.039	*The Manchester Regiment*	10/65	12/80

D50	45.040	*King's Shropshire Light Infantry*	5/65	
D52	45.123	*The Lancashire Fusiliers*	10/67	
D53	45.041	*Royal Tank Regiment*	9/64	
D54	45.023	*The Royal Pioneer Corps*	11/63	8/84
D55	45.144	*Royal Signals*	6/65	
D56	45.137	*The Bedfordshire & Hertfordshire Regiment (TA)*	12/62	
D58	45.043	*The King's Own Royal Border Regiment*	5/63	8/84
D59	45.104	*The Royal Warwickshire Fusiliers*	5/64	
D60	45.022	*Lytham St. Annes*	5/64	
D61	45.112	*Royal Army Ordnance Corps*	9/65	
D62	45.143	*5th Royal Inniskilling Dragoon Guards*	1/64	
D63	45.044	*Royal Inniskilling Fusilier*	10/65	
D64	45.045	*Coldstream Guardsman*	4/65	5/83
D65	45.111	*Grenadier Guardsman*	5/64	
D67	45.118	*The Royal Artilleryman*	10/65	
D68	45.046	*Royal Fusilier*	1/67	
D70	45.048	*The Royal Marines*	12/64	
D71	45.049	*The Staffordshire Regiment (The Prince of Wales's)*	5/66	
D77	45.004	*Royal Irish Fusilier*	9/65	
D84	45.055	*The Royal Corps of Transport*	6/66	
D89	45.006	*Honourable Artillery Company*	6/65	
D98	45.059	*Royal Engineer*	12/66	
D99	45.135	*3rd Carabinier*	12/65	
D100	45.060	*Sherwood Forester*	9/61	
D137	45.014	*The Cheshire Regiment*	6/66	
D163	46.026	*Leicestershire and Derbyshire Yeomanry*	4/62	11/84

ORIGINAL BR No	BR TOPS No	DATE IN SERVICE	Date Renumbered	Date Withdrawn	ORIGINAL BR No	BR TOPS No	DATE IN SERVICE	Date Renumbered	Date Withdrawn
D1	44.001	9/59	2/74	10/76	D64	45.045	4/62	2/75	
D2	44.002	10/59	3/74	4/79	D65	45.111	4/62	8/73	
D3	44.003	10/59	3/74	7/76	D66	45.146	4/62	12/74	
D4	44.004	10/59	4/74	11/80	D67	45.118	5/62	12/73	
D5	44.005	11/59	11/73	4/78	D68	45.046	10/60	2/75	
D6	44.006	12/59	10/73	1/77	D69	45.047	11/60	1/75	8/80
D7	44.007	12/59	2/74	11/80	D70	45.048	12/60	4/75	
D8	44.008	12/59	3/74	11/80	D71	45.049	12/60	3/75	
D9	44.009	12/59	2/74	5/79	D72	45.050	12/60	2/75	8/84
D10	44.010	2/60	2/74	5/77	D73	45.110	12/60	7/73	
D11	45.122	9/60	3/74		D74	45.051	12/60	1/75	
D12	45.011	10/60	2/74	5/81	D75	45.052	12/60	1/75	
D13	45.001	11/60	4/73		D76	45.053	1/61	3/75	11/83
D14	45.015	12/60	3/74		D77	45.004	1/61	9/73	
D15	45.018	12/60	7/74	1/81	D78	45.150	1/61	7/75	
D16	45.016	12/60	4/74		D79	45.005	1/61	11/73	
D17	45.024	1/61	4/75	12/80	D80	45.113	1/61	10/73	
D18	45.121	1/61	2/74		D81	45.115	1/61	10/73	
D19	45.025	1/61	2/75	5/81	D82	45.141	1/61	11/74	
D20	45.013	2/61	3/74		D83	45.142	1/61	11/74	
D21	45.026	2/61	2/75		D84	45.055	1/61	1/75	
D22	45.132	3/61	7/74		D85	45.109	2/62	7/73	
D23	45.017	4/61	4/74		D86	45.105	3/62	4/73	
D24	45.027	4/61	2/75	5/81	D87	45.127	2/62	5/74	
D25	45.021	4/61	10/74	12/80	D88	45.136	3/61	9/74	
D26	45.020	4/61	8/74		D89	45.006	3/61	11/73	
D27	45.028	5/61	3/75	1/81	D90	45.008	3/61	11/73	12/80
D28	45.124	5/61	4/74		D91	45.056	3/61	3/75	
D29	45.002	5/61	6/73	8/84	D92	45.138	3/61	10/74	
D30	45.029	5/61	4/75		D93	45.057	4/61	1/75	1/85
D31	45.030	6/61	2/75	11/80	D94	45.114	4/61	9/73	
D32	45.126	6/61	5/74		D95	45.054	4/61	1/75	1/85
D33	45.019	7/61	7/74	1/81	D96	45.101	4/61	3/73	
D34	45.119	7/61	1/74		D97	45.058	4/61	1/75	
D35	45.117	7/61	12/73		D98	45.059	5/61	1/75	
D36	45.031	7/61	5/75	5/81	D99	45.135	5/61	9/74	
D37	45.009	7/61	12/73		D100	45.060	5/61	1/75	
D38	45.032	7/61	2/75	12/80	D101	45.061	5/61	6/75	8/81
D39	45.033	8/61	1/75		D102	45.140	5/61	10/74	
D40	45.133	8/61	7/74		D103	45.062	6/61	1/75	
D41	45.147	8/61	1/75	1/85	D104	45.063	6/61	1/75	
D42	45.034	9/61	2/75		D105	45.064	6/61	1/75	1/85
D43	45.107	9/61	5/73		D106	45.106	6/61	5/73	
D44	45.035	9/61	2/75		D107	45.120	7/61	2/74	
D45	45.036	9/61	5/75	5/81	D108	45.012	8/61	3/74	
D46	45.037	10/61	1/75		D109	45.139	7/61	10/74	
D47	45.116	10/61	10/73		D110	45.065	8/61	1/75	
D48	45.038	10/61	3/75		D111	45.129	8/61	6/74	
D49	45.039	10/61	4/75	12/80	D112	45.010	8/61	12/73	
D50	45.040	6/62	1/75		D113	45.128	9/61	6/74	
D51	45.102	6/62	3/73		D114	45.066	9/61	2/75	
D52	45.123	6/62	4/74		D115	45.067	9/61	1/75	6/77
D53	45.041	7/62	5/75		D116	45.103	9/61	3/73	
D54	45.023	8/62	1/75	8/84	D117	45.130	9/61	6/74	
D55	45.144	10/62	12/74		D118	45.068	10/61	6/75	
D56	45.137	12/62	9/74		D119	45.007	10/61	11/73	
D57	45.042	7/63	12/74		D120	45.108	10/61	6/73	
D58	45.043	2/62	12/74	8/84	D121	45.069	10/61	1/75	
D59	45.104	2/62	4/73		D122	45.070	11/61	1/75	
D60	45.022	2/62	11/74		D123	45.125	11/61	4/74	
D61	45.122	3/62	8/73		D124	45.131	11/61	6/74	
D62	45.143	3/62	11/74		D125	45.071	11/61	12/75	7/81
D63	45.044	4/62	3/75		D126	45.134	12/61	8/74	

ORIGINAL BR No	BR TOPS No	DATE IN SERVICE	Date Renumbered	Date Withdrawn	ORIGINAL BR No	BR TOPS No	DATE IN SERVICE	Date Renumbered	Date Withdrawn
D127	45.072	12/61	1/75		D163	46.026	4/62	2/74	11/84
D128	45.145	12/61	12/74		D164	46.027	4/62	1/74	11/84
D129	45,073	12/61	2/75	10/81	D165	46.028	5/62	4/74	5/84
D130	45.148	12/61	1/75		D166	46.029	5/62	10/73	1/83
D131	45.074	12/61	1/75		D167	46.030	5/62	1/74	12/80
D132	45.075	12/61	2/75	1/85	D168	46.031	5/62	2/74	4/83
D133	45.003	1/62	6/73		D169	46.032	6/62	3/74	4/84
D134	45.076	1/62	1/75		D170	46.033	6/62	1/74	6/83
D135	45.149	1/62	2/75		D171	46.034	7/62	1/74	12/80
D136	45.077	1/62	1/75		D172	46.035	7/62	12/73	11/84
D137	45.014	1/62	3/74		D173	46.036	7/62	11/73	5/82
D138	46.001	11/61	2/74	12/81	D174	46.037	7/62	1/74	6/84
D139	46.002	11/61	2/74	9/81	D175	46.038	8/62	1/74	2/82
D140	46.003	12/61	2/74	10/78	D176	46.039	8/62	2/74	9/83
D141	46.004	12/61	1/74	6/83	D177	46.040	8/62	2/74	12/80
D142	46.005	1/62	2/74	12/77	D178	46.041	9/62	2/74	12/80
D143	46.006	12/61	2/74	1/82	D179	46.042	9/62	2/74	12/80
D144	46.007	1/62	1/74	2/82	D180	46.043	9/62	2/74	12/80
D145	46.008	1/62	9/73	10/81	D181	46.044	9/62	1/74	4/84
D146	46.009	1/62	9/73	11/83	D182	46.045	9/62	9/73	11/84
D147	46.010	1/62	4/74	10/84	D183	46.046	10/62	1/74	5/84
D148	46.011	1/62	1/74	11/84	D184	46.047	10/62	1/74	9/84
D149	46.012	1/62	1/74	7/80	D185	46.048	10/62	3/74	9/81
D150	46.013	2/62	1/74	8/80	D186	46.049	11/62	2/74	12/82
D151	46.014	1/62	12/73	5/84	D187	46.050	11/62	1/74	10/82
D152	46.015	2/62	5/74	12/80	D188	46.051	12/62	12/73	12/83
D153	46.016	2/62	4/74	12/83	D189	46.052	1/63	2/74	9/84
D154	46.017	2/62	1/74	4/84	D190	46.053	1/63	1/74	2/81
D155	46.018	2/62	2/74	12/83	D191	46.054	1/63	1/74	1/82
D156	46.019	2/62	3/74	12/80	D192	46.055	1/63	1/74	10/82
D157	46.020	3/62	2/74	12/80	D193	46.056	1/63	11/73	10/82
D158	46.021	3/62	2/74	1/83					
D159	46.022	3/62	2/74	3/82					
D160	46.023	4/62	3/74	12/83	D1-D49 built BR, Derby				
D161	46.024	4/62	1/74	4/78	D50-D137 built BR, Crewe				
D162	46.025	4/62	2/74	11/84	D138-D193 built BR, Derby				

Notes

D4   Preserved at Midland Railway Trust, Butterley

D8   Preserved at Strathspey Railway. Renamed
Schichallion

D57   Used for uprated power unit trials 12/62–7/63

46.009   to Departmental stock 11/83 as 97.401.
Destroyed in nuclear fuel flask collision test
17/7/84

46.023   to Departmental stock 12/83 as 97.402.
Withdrawn.

46.035   to Departmental stock 12/84 as 97.403

46.045   to Departmental stock 12/84 as 97.404

The following additional locomotives were withdrawn
in the period to June 1985:

45.010   3/85
45.065   3/85
45.042   4/85
45.055   4/85
45.072   4/85
45.038   6/85

Above: D1 at Cricklewood on 27 April 1959, some four months before officially entering traffic. The paintwork, 'ferret and dartboard' emblem and works plates are immaculate.
S. Lambert

Below: A front three-quarter view of D1 taken after construction at Derby Works. The nameplate, length and livery are clearly apparent. *BR (WR)*

Above: The body of D114 is lowered onto its bogies during construction at Derby in 1961. *Colin Marsden Collection*

*Below:*Derby Workshops in 1960, with Sulzer Type 2 and 4 locomotives under construction. Type 2 bogies and a twin-bank Type 4 engine are in the foreground *Colin Marsden Collection*

Above: Eight 'Peaks' under construction at Derby during 1960. The boards on each locomotove refer to 'Co-Co class diesel' – a reminder of the original choice of wheel arrangement for the 'Peaks'. *BR(LMR)*

Below: Two newly-built 'Peaks' undergo train heating boiler tests at Crewe Works. *J.R. Carter*

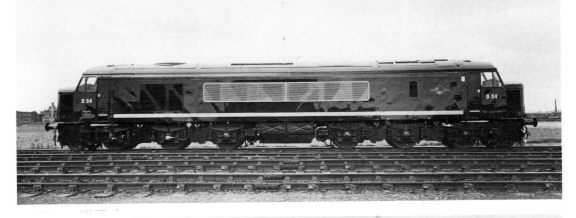

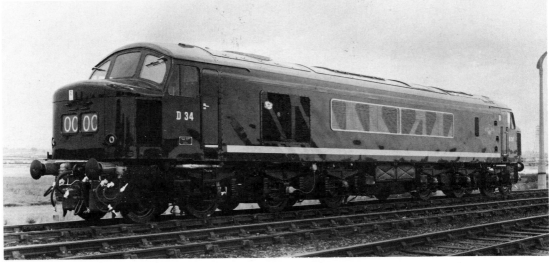

Top: Two views of D34 as built at Derby in 1961. A broadside viewpoint showing most of the body features. *Colin Marsden Collection*

Above: . . . and a three-quarter view illustrating the two-piece centre route indicator panel fitted after end doors were abolished. *BR(WR)*

Below: D9 *Snowdon* at Whiteacre Junction, between Nuneaton and Birmingham in June 1967. *D. Birch*

Above: After a brief spell on the WCML, the first 10 'Peaks' were relegated to freight work from Toton yard. D8 *Penyghent* passes Leicester with a Toton-Brent coal train on 1 July 1969. *J.H. Cooper-Smith*

Below: D1 *Scafell Pike* and D2 *Helvellyn* head south with a coal train near Barrow-on-Soar in the summer of 1967. D1 has lost the cover above the water filling point, and the bodyside steps remain accessible. The boiler would be out of use by this time. D2 retains her original livery. *G. Wignall*

Above: The 16.45 Manchester Central–London St Pancras crosses Chinley South Junction behind D86 on 21 May 1966. The Midland route to Manchester was the first regular mainline duty which the 'Peaks' operated for a considerable length of time. *B. Stephenson*

Below: By the mid-1970s the 'Thames–Clyde Express' title had disappeared, although the services still operated. The down train passes the site of Apperley Bridge Station behind No 45.021 on 4 June 1976. *G.W. Morrison*

Below: Holbeck's D23 crosses Lunds viaduct, between Ais Gill and Garsdale, with the up 'Waverley' express on 23 June 1964. *M. York*

Bottom: D23 seen again, four years later and still carrying a Holbeck shed plate. In rather more typical Settle & Carlisle summer weather conditions, the locomotive is hauling the up 'Thames–Clyde Express' past the closed Dent Head signal box on 11 August 1968. *D. Wharton*

Left: Derby-built D182 hauls a mixed bag of stock forming the 11.05 Newcastle–York parcels below the NER signal box at Church Street, West Hartlepool, on 8 June 1967. All the Class 46 locomotives were built with the central one-piece headcode panel as shown. *J.M. Boyes*

Bottom left: A named but unidentified 'Peak' hauls the 16.35 Glasgow–Inverness east of Gleneagles on 28 May 1966. *C.W.R. Bowman*

Top right: D73 passes a collection of ex-LMS and ex-MR signals at Kibworth on 18 June 1967 with a Sheffield–St Pancras express. *J.H. Cooper-Smith*

Centre right: Due to a freight train derailment on the Settle & Carlisle at Stainforth, D159 was diverted via the WCML with the down 'Thames–Clyde Express' on 9 May 1963. The train is seen here amidst the barren surroundings of Shap Wells. *Noel A. Machell*

Bottom: Class 44 No 44.008 (formerly *Penyghent*) passes Foxlow Junction, near Staveley, with a Bescot-Tinsley freight on 23 May 1978. A Class 20 disappears around the corner with empty wagons for Markham Colliery. *A.R. Kaye*

Above: Two scenes at Derby: D102 prepares to leave with a Newcastle–Bristol express on 8 June 1968.

Below: ... and later in the day, D181 stands in the station with the 10.30 Bristol–Newcastle. This locomotive displays rail blue livery, all-over yellow cab ends and later style numerals placed behind the cab. *Both D. Wharton*

Right: Class 45/1 No 45.112 sweeps through Ambergate with the 12.10 Sheffield–St Pancras express on 24 January 1976. The line on the left is the remains of the former Derby–Manchester route, scene of many early 'Peak' activities, now reduced to a single-line branch to Matlock. *L.A. Nixon*

Above: Class 45/1 No 45.140 accelerates away from Nottingham with the 15.10 to St Pancras on 21 May 1977. These accelerated services using Mk II coaching stock, were an arduous duty on which the 'Peaks' acquitted themselves well. This particular locomotive is displaying a rather unusual headcode! *D. Hayes*

Below: Their mixed-traffic origin has always ensured 'Peaks' can perform equally well on all varieties of freight haulage. Class 45/0 No 45.073 takes a southbound MGR train past Finedon Rd, Wellingborough on 2 June 1977. *K. Lane*

Left: Class 46 No D179 awaits departure from Bristol with the 13.20 Newcastle train on 31 October 1968. *P.J. Fowler*

Below: Diesel-electric and diesel-hydraulic meet at Cogload Junction D16 hauls the 10.16 Manchester (Piccadilly)–Plymouth above an unidentified 'Western' class locomotive on the up 'Cornish Riviera Limited' on 10 March 1973. *P.J. Fowler*

Bottom: A 'Peak' in the heart of Devon. Class 46 No 185 approaches Tiverton Junction on 8 September 1973 with the Leeds–Paignton 'Devonian'. *P.D. Hawkins*

Top left: No 45.126 accelerates away from Totnes with a down inter-regional express on 4 August 1975. *B. Morrison*

Above left: The solitary named Class 46 machine, No 46.026 *Leicestershire and Derbyshire Yeomanry* enters Totnes station with an up perishables train on 4 August 1975. *B. Morrison*

Left: Exeter (St Davids) station appears deserted as No 46.004 pauses with the 06.42 Leeds–Paignton on 13 July 1976. *B. Morrison*

Above: Class 46 No 46.034 enters Exeter (St Davids) with the 15.10 Plymouth–Manchester (Piccadilly) on 21 July 1977. This view clearly shows the engine exhaust outlet, train heating boiler exhaust, engine access covers and former water filling point. *B. Morrison*

Right: One of south Devon's most famous railway photographic locations – Class 46 No 46.010 passes along the coast near Dawlish with the 08.45 Liverpool–Penzance on 9 September 1978. The 'domino' in the route indicator was a common feature in the last days before the central boxes were removed altogether.
A. Wynne

Top right: Class 45 No 50 *The King's Shropshire Light Infantry* pauses at Newcastle with the 07.20 York–Aberdeen on 3 April 1971. The train heating boiler water supply is being replenished by the solebar level filling point fitted to replace the original roof-mounted point. *I.S. Carr*

Right: After conversion to Class 45/1, No 45.150 is seen here double-heading the 08.01 Manchester–St Pancras with No 45.108 at Cossington on 5 July 1975. The purpose of the working was to give No 45.150 a test run from Derby to Leicester, the locomotive returning light engine later in the day. The new ETH plug and socket are clearly visible. *D. Clow*

Below: Class 45/1 No 45.128 passes Beeston, near Nottingham, with an unidentified up express on 3 April 1977. Note the unusual headcode panel arrangement. *D. Hayes*

Above: Engineering work on the Midland route between Sheffield and Chesterfield often results in trains being diverted along the 'Old Road', the ex-North Midland Railway route via Renishaw and Woodhouse. Class 46 No 46.007 approaches Foxlow Junction, near Staveley, with a diverted Leeds–Bristol train on 19 March 1978.   *T. Dodgson*

Below: Class 45/1 No 45.120 arrives at Loughborough with the 13.12 Nottingham–St Pancras on 31 March 1978.   *C.J. Tuffs*

Above: A Nottingham–St Pancras express approaches Loughborough on 29 May 1978 hauled by No 45.118 *The Royal Artilleryman.* G.W. Morrison

Below: Two Class 45/0 locomotives at Wigston South Junction, near Leicester; No 45015 comes off the Nuneaton line and heads south with a ballast train, whilst an unidentified member of the class (fitted with the final front end arrangement) awaits its next turn of duty. *L.A. Nixon*

Below Class 45/0 No 45.036 accelerates a down express away from Rotherham (Masboro') on 12 February 1977.   *L.A. Nixon*

Bottom: A 'Peak' on a service which no longer exists – No 45.009 nears Shipley with the 08.00 St Pancras–Glasgow on 24 April 1976.   *M. Hall*

Above: Snow covered Pen-y-Ghent provides a spectacular background to 'Peak' No 44 heading north at Ribblehead with the down 'Thames–Clyde Express' on 2 March 1974. *J.H. Cooper-Smith*

Right: Two days later, the southbound train passes below a snow-dusted Wild Boar Fell at Ais Gill Summit behind 'Peak' No 49 *The Manchester Regiment*. These un-prefixed numbers were carried by BR diesel and electric locomotives for varying periods of time between the demise of steam power and the implementation of the TOPS scheme. No 49 was renumbered 45.039 in 1975 and subsequently withdrawn in December 1980. *J.H. Cooper-Smith*

Above: A scene which the assembled gathering of photographers at Armathwaite was definitely not expecting! On a beautiful autumn day in 1981, several dozen enthusiasts were eagerly watching the approach of No 46229 *Duchess of Hamilton* when No 45.033 drifted into the viewfinder with a northbound coal train, completely changing the planned scene and causing much gnashing of teeth! *S.R. Batty*

Below: Freight traffic has now disappeared from the Settle & Carlisle and the train of 16 ton unbraked mineral wagons has now all but vanished from the BR scene. 'Peak' No 45.042 approaches Ais Gill summit with a train of coal empties returning from Scotland to Yorkshire on 16 March 1975. *P.J. Robinson*

Left: An unidentified 'Peak' approaches Salt Lake City, near Ribblehead, with the 09.01 Leeds–Glasgow on 31 January 1976.
L.A. Nixon

Bottom: The end of an era. Holbeck 'Peak' No 45.073 hauls the last up 'Thames–Clyde Express' from Glasgow to St Pancras through the splendid Midland Railway station buildings at Hellifield on 2 May 1976.
G.W. Morrison

Right: A Nottingham–Glasgow service remained in place of the withdrawn St Pancras trains, until these too were withdrawn in 1982. An unidentified 'Peak' passes the now demolished water tower at Blea Moor with the 10.25 Nottingham–Glasgow on 9 August 1979.   *C.F. Burton*

Below right: Sunlight and shadow at Manchester (Piccadilly) on 16 August 1975. 'Peak' No 45.049 *The Staffordshire Regiment (The Prince of Wales's)* leaves with the 18.06 for St Pancras, whilst Class 86 electric No 86.208 awaits departure with the 18.10 for Euston. A Class 40 can be seen to the left of the 'Peak'.
D. Griffiths

Above: 'Peaks' have been occasional performers on the Harwich–Manchester service, and here Class 46 No 46.012 is seen crossing Marple Viaduct, on the approach to Manchester, in June 1976. This 'Peak' was withdrawn in July 1980. *F. Wilde ARPS*

Below: Class 45/0 No 45.052 rounds Buxworth curve, near Chinley, with the 14.25 Blackpool (North)–Leicester on 15 July 1978.   *L.A. Nixon*

Above: Two views of Class 44 No 44.008 (formerly *Penyghent*) during the last 18 months of its operational life. Here it is seen near Westhouses hauling the 18.15 Spondon–Tinsley goods on 15 June 1979. The painted wheel tyres, depot name on the bufferbeam and immaculate paintwork are a reflection of Toton depot's care of the Class 44 machines. *L.P. Gater*

Above: Just over three months later, No 44.008 is seen on 28 September working the 06.20 Goole–Wolverhampton steel coil train. The intervening weeks have seen more paint applied to the roof, and also the restoration of the original waist-level band. *B.J. Nicolle*

Below: Class 45/0 No 45.001 leaves Teignmouth with an Eastern Region express on 8 August 1975. Built as D13 and originally fitted with end doors and split box route indicators, this view shows the modified pattern fitted before the final design of front end, incorporating two marker lights, was fitted. *B. Morrison*

Above: Two views of the 07.47 Penzance–Liverpool in 1979 Class 46 No 46.025 shuts off power for the approach to Taunton on 13 July,

Below: ...and on 4 October No 45.019 arrives at Totnes. *Both L. Bertram*

Left: Near Stenson Junction, between Derby and Tamworth. Class 20s Nos 20.143 and 20.171 plod along with a coal train as Class 46 No 46.044 flies past on a Newcastle–Bristol express on 20 July 1977. *D. Clow*

Below: No 45.070 clears Milford Junction with the 11.45 Cardiff–Newcastle on 2 April 1979. *S.R. Batty*

Right: The trans-Pennine services via Manchester and Leeds are a 'Peak' stronghold, with the occasional Class 47 in evidence. No 45.052 sweeps through Greenfield, between Diggle and Stalybridge, with the 10.02 Newcastle–Liverpool on 10 June 1976.   *D.A. Flitcroft*

Below: Class 46 No 46.034 approaches Standedge tunnel at Diggle with the 10.10 Liverpool–Newcastle on 10 June 1976. The tunnel in the background gave access to the Micklehurst loop, closed completely in the 1960s and now lifted.   *D.A. Flitcroft*

Above: The eastern end of Standedge tunnel, with a Class 46 about to enter with the 10.02 Newcastle–Liverpool on 8 July 1976.   *D.A. Flitcroft*

Below: With power shut off for the descent to Stalybridge, 'Peak' No 46.039 heads the 09.42 Newcastle–Manchester (Victoria) past Lydgate, near Greenfield, on 15 October 1977.   *D.A. Flitcroft*

Above: The 09.35 Newcastle–Liverpool passes Greenfield on 28 May 1978 behind Class 46 No 46.051.   *D.A. Flitcroft*

Below: A summer Saturday Weymouth–Bradford train pauses at Huddersfield on 17 August 1978. 'Peak' No 45.032 (now withdrawn) will run round its train before departure via Bradley Wood and Greetland to Halifax.   *A.R. Kaye*

Above:'Peak' No 105 (now 45.064) in Derby Workshops on 23 March 1969. At this time the locomotive had different headcode panels at each end (No 1 end carried a single central panel), one of a few locomotives to have this combination at some stage of their lives. *D.L. Percival*

Left: Maintenance work at Toton TMD – a Sulzer LDA piston and connecting rod asembly receives attention. *BR (LMR)*

Below: Cab assemblies from Nos 45.071 and 45.051 amidst various auxiliary motors inside Derby workshops, 22 November 1975. *B. Morrison*

Left: A 'Peak' bogie receives attention at Toton TMD.
BR (LMR)

Below: Saltley TMD on 22 May 1975, with Class 45/0
No 45.059 *Royal Engineer* at rest.   *P.D. Hawkins*

Right: Chesterfield's crooked spire is prominent in the
background of this view of Class 45/1 No 45.128 hauling the
07.50 St Pancras–Sheffield on 30 January 1980.
C.J. Marsden

Below right: Fine weather at Finedon as Class 45/1 No 45.131
speeds along with the 14.07 Derby–St Pancras on 16 May
1980.   *C.J. Marsden*

Above: Light and shade at Luton on 7 February 1981. Class 45/0 No 45.049 *The Staffordshire Regiment (The Prince of Wales's)* is held at signals with a loaded MGR train as a St Pancras DMU departs from the station. *A.N. Pierce*

Below: Class 45/1 No 45.110, complete with waist-level band, leaves Nottingham with the 18.48 for St Pancras on 6 April 1980. *L. Bertram*

Above: The 'Peaks' are regularly used for the haulage of stone trains from the East Midlands. No 45.029 is seen here passing below the wires at Chalton, north of Luton, with such a train on 11 May 1981. *L. Bertram*

Below: A long string of loaded Redland stone hoppers is hauled past Finedon Road box on 20 August 1982 by Nos 45.002 and 45.003. *M. Ricks*

Top right: A Plymouth express is accelerated away from Chesterfield by Class 46 No 46.031 on 12 September 1981. *C.J. Marsden*

Right: No 45.049 again, seen here hauling an up freight near Rearsby, between Leicester and Melton Mowbray. *M. Mitchell*

Below: Class 46 No 46.026 *Leicestershire and Derbyshire Yeomanry* awaits departure from Sheffield with a football supporters' excursion to London on 16 April 1983. Points of interest here are the steam escaping from the train heating boiler, and the Gateshead coat of arms above the cabside number.
G.S. Cutts

Above: Booked double-heading is a rare occurence, but one such example in 1983 was to be found on the Sundays 13.05 Nottingham–St Pancras. Here Nos 45.126 and 45.123 pass Barrow-on-Soar on 10 July 1983. *M. Mitchell*

Below: The impressive collection of semaphore signals at Goose Hill Junction, Normanton, is alas no longer present. 'Peak' No 45.064 hauls a short ballast train from the Wakefield line towards the station in the summer of 1981. *S.R. Batty*

Above: Class 45/0 No 45.004 *Royal Irish Fusilier* leaves Steeton level crossing, near Keighley, with a Carlisle–Healey Mills freight on 16 February 1981.   *T. Hanson*

Below: The 11.50 Glasgow–Nottingham express approaches Ais Gill summit behind 'Peak' No 45.050 in July 1981.
S.R. Batty

Top: The bulk of Whernside towers above No 45.059 *Royal Engineer* passing Ribblehead station with the 10.00 Carlisle–Leeds on 25 September 1982. *G.S. Cutts*

Above: With a somewhat buckled front end in view, No 45.055 *Royal Corps of Transport* passes the remains of Ais Gill signalbox with the 11.50 Glasgow–Nottingham on 27 April 1982. *J.S. Whiteley*

Above: Gateshead Class 46 No 46.051 passes the remains of Newbiggin station with the 16.37 Carlisle–Leeds on 22 October 1983. Although 'Peaks' monopolised the Leeds–Carlisle services for many years, they now share the much-reduced service with Classes 31 and 47. *S.R. Batty*

Below: The 09.07 Leeds–Carlisle approaches Blea Moor behind Class 45/1 No 45.146 on 5 November 1983. *S.R. Batty*

Below: All-out-effort: No 45.071 attacks the Lickey incline with a heavy stone train, assised in the rear by a pair of Class 37 locomotives. *I.J. Hodson*

Bottom: Photographed barely six months before withdrawal, Class 45/0 No 45.018 is seen near Trulefoot with the 12.12 Penzance–Crewe train on 23 August 1980. *C.J. Marsden*

Above: Class 45/0 No 45.036 passes beneath some ex-GWR semaphore signals at Aller Junction on 8 July 1980 whilst hauling the 10.23 Manchester (Piccadilly)–Plymouth. *B. Morrison*

Right: The only named Class 46 No 46.026 *Leicestershire and Derbyshire Yeomanry* leaves Dawlish Warren station with a Saturdays only Wolverhampton–Paignton train on 23 August 1980. *C.J. Marsden*

Above: 'Peak' No 45.014 (formerly *The Cheshire Regiment*) speeds through Exminster with the Sundays 16.25 Paignton–Derby on 13 September 1981. *G.F. Gillham*

Below: Class 45/0 No 45.017 starts away from a signal check at Aller Junction on 11 January 1982 with a mixed freight train. Class 47 Nos 47.463 and 47.171 pass behind on a snowplough working. *M.S. Wilkins*

Above: The 09.05 St Blazey-Severn Tunnel Junction, formed of one Railfreight VDA van and three Polybulk wagons passes Brent behind No 45.075 on 16 September 1982. *C.J. Marsden*

Below: An ETH-fitted 'Peak' on a partially-braked freight train – Class 45/1 No 45.129 bowls along the down main near Wootton Bassett in April 1983. *S.R. Batty*

Above: One of the very few passenger trains to traverse the curve between Gascoigne Wood, on the Selby–Leeds line, and Milford Junction on the NESW line between Church Fenton and Pontefract. No 45.103 eases the summer Saturdays only 14.04 Scarborough–Luton round the curve on 20 August 1983. *S.R. Batty*

Left: A shortage of HST sets led to some advertised services being turned over to locomotive-hauled stock from July 1983. Class 45/1 No 45.118 *The Royal Artilleryman* hauls the 12.30 Leeds–Cardiff into Ardsley tunnel, between Leeds and Wakefield, on 18 August 1983. *S.R. Batty*

Above: On a freezing day in December 1981 with heavy snowfall imminent, No 45.004 *Royal Irish Fusilier* hurries the Heysham–Haverton Hill ammonia tanks towards Melling tunnel.
S.R. Batty

Right: Class 46 No 46.035 approaches Newcastle (Central) with empty coaching stock from Heaton on 14 May 1977.   *G. W. Morrison*

Above: Class 45/0 No 45.026 caught in the morning sunshine at Healey Mills. *S.R. Batty*

Left: The Foss Island branch, York, on 21 May 1978. 'Peak' No 45.024 (withdrawn in October 1980) is in charge of an engineers' train at Rowntree's Halt, with Class 37 No 37.102 in the background. *E.A.J. Saunders*

Bottom left: No 45.063 speeds along the Calder Valley near Thornhill with an ECS working for Manchester (Red Bank) on a spring day in 1982. *S.R. Batty*

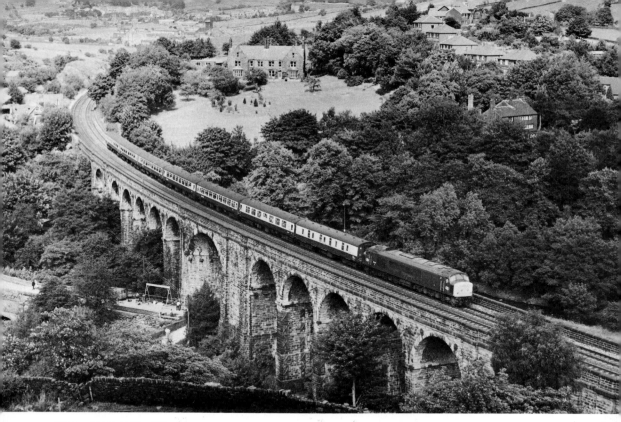

Left: The 12.57 Scarborough–Bangor sweeps across Saddleworth viaduct behind Class 45/1 No 45.129 on 12 August 1983. *S.R. Batty*

Below left: Class 46 locomotives are no longer seen on the trans-Pennine service, in stark contrast to their monopoly of the route in earlier years. Gateshead depot's No 46.039 enters Leeds with the 14.05 Liverpool–Newcastle on 23 August 1983. This locomotive was withdrawn from service during the following month. *S.R. Batty*

Above: Heaton Lodge Junction, between Mirfield and Huddersfield, has been greatly remodelled since the closure of the bulk of the Leeds 'New Line' in the mid-1960s. Class 45/1 No 45.137 *The Bedfordshire and Hertfordshire Regiment (TA)* swings off the last remaining section of the 'New Line' and crosses the new alignment onto the ex-LYR line at Heaton Lodge with the 11.15 Bangor–Scarborough on 24 October 1983. *S.R. Batty*

Below: Class 45/1 No 45.125 passes Heaton Lodge South Junction (formerly Spen Valley Junction) with the 09.15 Bangor–Scarborough on 19 October 1983. *S.R. Batty*

Above: The 09.22 Newcastle–Liverpool heads for Heaton Lodge South Junction behind class 45/1 No 45.112 *The Royal Army Ordnance Corps* on 24 October 1983.   *S.R. Batty*

Below: Class 45/1 No 45.150 leaves Huddersfield and approaches Deighton with the 09.05 Liverpool–Scarborough on 16 April 1984.   *S.R. Batty*

Above right: No 45.140 climbs towards Standedge tunnel with the 11.22 Newcastle–Liverpool on 19 October 1984. *S.R. Batty*

Right: The 12.05 Liverpool–Scarborough approaches Paddock, on the descent to Huddersfield, behind Class 45/1 No 45.135 on 19 October 1983. These trans-Pennine duties do not often exceed seven vehicles, but the locomotive diagrams are intensive and demand high availability.   *S.R. Batty*

Above: Two views of 'Peaks' at Marsden, close to the eastern portal of Standedge tunnel. Here, No 45.115 passes the station with the 09.22 Newcastle–Liverpool on 16 April 1984.

Below: ... and a few moments later, the Pennine Spring sunshine graces No 45.139 hauling the 09.15 Bangor–Scarborough around the curves towards the station. *Both S.R. Batty*

Top: The gloom of Standedge tunnel gives way to autumn sunlight as 45.125 emerges with the 10.05 Liverpool–Newcastle on 21 October 1983. *S.R. Batty*

Above: The descent from Standedge to Stalybridge includes many sweeping curves. No 45.113 passes the site of Diggle Junction on 21 October 1983 with the 11.00 Scarborough–Bangor. *S.R. Batty*

Above: Class 45/1 No 45.143 *5th Royal Inniskilling Dragoon Guards* climbs up the last stretch towards Diggle with the 12.05 Liverpool–Scarborough on 16 April 1984.   *S.R. Batty*

Below: The 12.57 Scarborough–Bangor nears Mossley behind Class 45/1 No 45.127 on 3 March 1984.   *S.R. Batty*

Below: 'Peak' No 45.120 emerges from Scout tunnel with the 11.22 Newcastle–Liverpool on 16 April 1984.   *S.R. Batty*

Bottom: The closed Hartshead power station dominates this view of a 'Peak' hauling the 14.05 Liverpool–Newcastle past the site of Black Rock signal box on 16 April 1984.   *S.R. Batty*

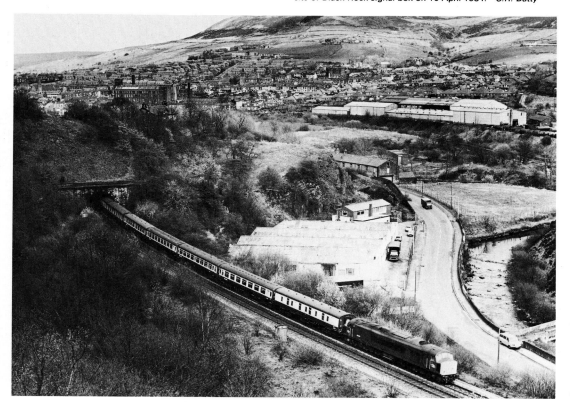

Above: Class 45/0 No 45.039 (formerly *The Manchester Regiment* and withdrawn in December 1980) bowls along the Castleford line at Milford Junction with a NESW line express in spring 1980. Soon afterwards all expresses were diverted via Pontefract, and then had to slow to use the double cross-over seen in the foreground. From May 1984, all NE–SW traffic was diverted again, to run from York to Sheffield via Doncaster and the ECML. *S.R. Batty*

Below: Burton Salmon was the junction of the Sheffield–Pontefract–York and Castleford–York routes. Class 45/0 No 45.048 *The Royal Marines* comes off the Pontefract line and heads for York with an inter regional express on 27 October 1981. Today, the two routes separate at Milford Junction and no trace of the former layout at Burton Salmon remains. *A. McKenna*

Right: Class 45/0 No 45.002 leaves Brotherton tunnel, on the York–Sheffield route, with the 14.23 Newcastle–Paignton on 13 August 1983. *S.R. Batty*

Below right: The 09.40 Poole–Newcastle accelerates away from Milford Junction behind Class 45/1 No 45.113 on 20 August 1983. *S.R. Batty*

Left: 'Peak' No 45.148 picks up after negotiating the crossovers at Milford with the 09.50 Newcastle–Poole on 26 August 1983. *S.R. Batty*

Centre left: An HST forming the 07.20 Penzance–Edinburgh speeds into view as No 45.117 approaches Milford with the 14.23 York–Plymouth on 17 September 1983. The latter was advertised as an HST service running via Leeds, but shortage of HST sets resulted in replacement by locomotive-hauled stock and, more often than not, 'Peak' power. *S.R. Batty*

Bottom left: In early 1984 the Plymouth train was retimed to leave York at 14.28. No 45.150 takes the train towards Pontefract (via the Swinton & Knottingley) at Milford junction on 6 March 1984. *S.R. Batty*

Above right: 'Peaks' at York. Class 45/1 No 45.148 moves the 09.50 Newcastle–Poole towards Holgate Road on 25 August 1982...

Right: ...and No 45.125 pauses in the station with a Liverpool–Newcastle express on the evening of 17 November 1980. *Both A. McKenna*

Below: Beneath an indifferent summer sky, No 45.111 *Grenadier Guardsman* speeds down Micklefield bank towards Church Fenton with the 14.05 Liverpool–Newcastle on 3 August 1983. *S.R. Batty*

Bottom: Class 45/1 No 45.123 *The Lancashire Fusilier* passes Neville Hill West Junction, Leeds, with the 09.05 Liverpool–Newcastle on 18 August 1983. *S.R. Batty*

Right: 'Peak' No 45.149 eases the summer Saturdays only 14.04 Scarborough–Luton off the swing bridge and through Selby station along the ECML, before taking the Leeds line at the southern end of the station. The train will proceed via Gascoigne Wood and then to Sheffield. This section of the ECML is now replaced by the Selby diversion route. *S.R. Batty*

Bottom right: Micklefield Junction is the point where the York and Selby lines converge for the remainder of the journey to Leeds. Class 45/1 No 45.134 heads westwards with the 11.00 Scarborough–Bangor on 6 December 1983. This locomotive is one of the few still to carry the remains of lamp attachments on the cab front. *S.R. Batty*

Above: Looking in the opposite direction on the same day, Class 45/1 No 45.146 takes the York line at over 60mph with the 10.05 Liverpool–Newcastle.   *S.R. Batty*

Below: The first snows of Winter at Ulleskelf are disturbed by No 45.134 hauling the 09.22 Newcastle–Liverpool on 12 December 1983.   *S.R. Batty*

Above right: 'Peak' No 45.141 approaches Cross Gates, on the outskirts of Leeds, with the 08.05 Liverpool–Newcastle on 31 March 1984.   *S.R. Batty*

Right: After a brief call at Malton, No 45.139 moves the 09.30 Llandudno–Scarborough onto the last leg of the journey on 4 May 1984.   *S.R. Batty*

Above: Departing with the 12.57 for Bangor, No 45.118 *The Royal Artilleryman* leaves Scarborough and passes Falsgrave signalbox on 4 May 1984.   *S.R. Batty*

Below: Waiting for signals – Class 45/0 No 45.041 *Royal Tank Regiment.*   *S.R. Batty*

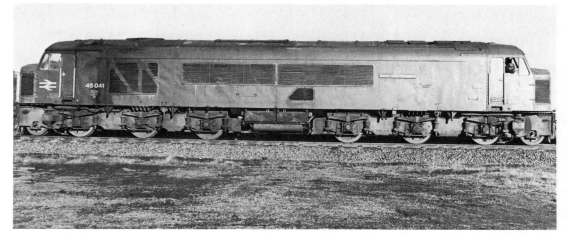